© 2021 Sunbird Books, an imprint of Phoenix International Publications, Inc.

8501 West Higgins Road   59 Gloucester Place
Chicago, Illinois 60631   London W1U 8JJ

www.sunbirdkidsbooks.com

Sunbird Books and the colophon are trademarks of Phoenix International Publications, Inc.

Library of Congress Control Number: 2020945233

ISBN: 978-1-5037-5708-0 Printed in China

Illustrations created digitally. Type is set in Billy and Myriad Pro.

A Wisdom
of Wombats

More Collective Animal Nouns and
the Meanings Behind Them

Written by Kathy Broderick
Illustrated by David DePasquale

sunbird books

a wisdom of wombats

wisdom \WIZ-dum\ *noun* : the ability to use experience and knowledge with common sense and insight

an aurora of polar bears

aurora \uh-ROR-uh\ *noun* : sunrise; daybreak

a bouquet of hummingbirds

bouquet \boo-KAY\ *noun* : an arrangement of flowers that is often given as a gift

a journey of giraffes

journey \JER-nee\ *noun* : the act of traveling
from one place to another; a trip

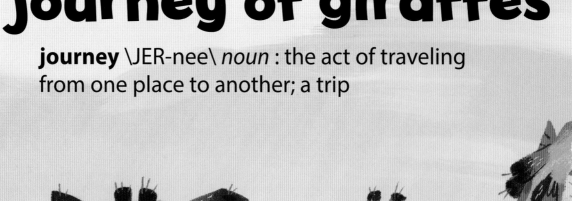

a constellation of sea stars

constellation \kahn-stuh-LAY-shun\ *noun* : a configuration of stars as seen from the earth

a gaze of raccoons

gaze \GAYZ\ *noun* : a long, fixed look; a stare

a troop of kangaroos

troop \TROOP\ *noun* : a group of persons or things that are part of a bigger organization

an obstinacy of buffalo

obstinacy \AHB-stin-uh-see\ *noun* : the quality of being hard to handle; stubbornness

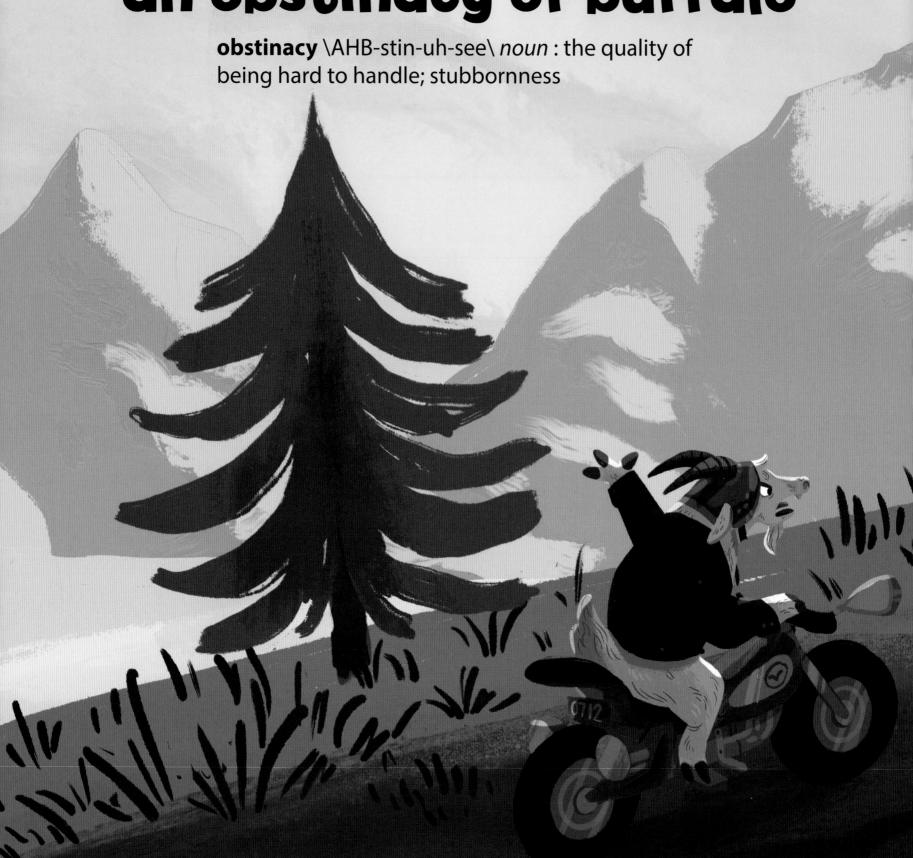

a gaggle of geese

gaggle \GAG-ul\ *noun* : a noisy group

a knot of toads

knot \NAHT\ *noun* : something that is twisted and looped upon itself

a race of roadrunners

race \RAYSS\ *noun* : a contest of speed

CRASH!

a crash of rhinoceroses

crash \KRASH\ *noun* : a sudden, loud sound

a school of fish

school \SKOOL\ *noun* : a place to go to learn

a squadron of pelicans

squadron \SKWAH-drun\ *noun* : a military
unit consisting of two or more soldiers

a surfeit of skunks

surfeit \SER-fit\ *noun* : an excess amount

a rumba of rattlesnakes

rumba \RUM-buh\ *noun* : a ballroom
dance based on a Cuban folk dance